# Sublunary Musings

# Sublunary Musings

Poems by

Carrie Weinberger

© 2024 Carrie Weinberger. All rights reserved.
This material may not be reproduced in any form, published,
reprinted, recorded, performed, broadcast,
rewritten, or redistributed without
the explicit permission of Carrie Weinberger.
All such actions are strictly prohibited by law.

Cover design by Shay Culligan
Cover image by Vizerskaya
Author photo by Jeff Weinberger

ISBN: 978-1-63980-568-6
Library of Congress Control Number: 2024908220

Kelsay Books
502 South 1040 East, A-119
American Fork, Utah 84003
Kelsaybooks.com

*for Jeff*

# Acknowledgments

Thankful acknowledgment to the editors of the following journals, in which some of the poems in this collection first appeared:

*California Quarterly*
*Channel*
*East on Central*
*The Last Stanza*
*The Light Ekphrastic*
*Raven's Perch*
*San Diego Poetry Annual*
*Summations*
*Talking River Review*

With special gratitude for the wisdom I draw from my poet sherpas, Joan Gerstein, Kate Harding, Amanda Mattimoe, and Kathy O'Fallon.

For my voluntary publicist, Donna Jacobsen, and for all of those friends who have embraced the poems in me.

# Contents

## Perigee

| | |
|---|---|
| A Visitation | 15 |
| Outsider Among Nuns | 16 |
| Incidentally | 17 |
| Back to the Land | 18 |
| Symmetry | 19 |
| Amoretti | 20 |
| Flight Lesson | 21 |
| He's No Equestrian | 22 |
| On Vermeer's *Woman in Blue, Reading a Letter* | 23 |
| Talking to Age | 24 |
| Measures of Infinity | 25 |
| Remedy for the Discomforts of Writing Poems | 26 |

## Apogee

| | |
|---|---|
| Shifty Words: A Sonnet | 29 |
| Annotations on Being Alone | 30 |
| Re-formation | 31 |
| Mary | 32 |
| Reasons for Shoes | 33 |
| Where Girls May Go | 34 |
| Shadow Horses | 35 |
| Almost Grief | 36 |
| En Passant | 37 |
| Consolation for Lost Love | 38 |
| He Said | 39 |
| Unweeding | 40 |
| A Taste of Tangerine | 41 |
| Okanagan Cradling Time | 42 |
| Not Now Keats's Autumn | 43 |
| Fractal Homily | 44 |

Earthshine

| | |
|---|---|
| Stoical Gardening | 47 |
| From the Altar of the Northern White Rhinos | 48 |
| Habitats | 49 |
| Death of the Sweet Peas: A Love Story | 50 |
| Large Language and Smashing Rocks | 51 |
| Inseparable | 52 |
| Coyote Reditus | 53 |
| To Live in the World | 54 |
| Equation | 55 |
| Fields and Trees | 56 |
| The Way to Eat a Pomegranate | 57 |
| To Love a "Super Mutt" | 58 |
| How to Rock and Roll with God | 59 |

Perigee

# A Visitation

When I changed my life, my roof blew off,
and I was speechless. Things fell in, sunlight
and rain, crow feathers and pine cones,
winged seeds and star dust, dry leaves and petals.
I listened to the wind, and had nothing to say.

The moon took notice of my open house, dropped in
one night for tea, and beaming profusely, melted all
the fallen things into the sounds of words. The moon
withdrew, and in the glow of my roofless room,
I began to speak.

# Outsider Among Nuns

They are what I want to be, made of steel simplicity,
and knowing that I won't be, let me tag along anyway,
a refugee from the outer place they also fled.
With eager gratitude, I weed the chapel garden,
and go boldly into wet woods, to clean the graves
under a mesh of tree boughs.

Rain fell through, tap tapped here and there
on fallen leaves, and former fallen leaves, mulching
all into a sweet fragrance of decay.

I did not pray for the dead sisters who, bedded down
side by side in silent absorption, all appetites surrendered
to perpetuity, wanted for nothing from those above ground
and hungry.

One late night in Rome, a church with doors opened to the street.
Inside, a stadium of candle flames, and I, a foreigner alone
in dark hours, seated my appeal among them, to hug that blaze.

So it was, when those nuns in denim habits showed up
where the graves and I were, bringing potato chips,
*Lays* hosts for all, a welcome dry wafer on the tongue in rain,
communion in that rapture of a salty crisp crush in the mouth
it's just human to love.

# Incidentally

>owing to my grandmother

Growling planes plough her sky, and the doe-eyed girl
takes refuge in a cathedral. Fresh, incongruous in those
stone cold shadows as the trembling daffodils among
sarcophagi of long dead knights like self-embracing men
asleep in trenches.

When she steps outside in startling light, a silent soldier stoops
to tie her bootlace. The same sun warms her hair as seeps into
his neck, the grey wool of his coat, the smooth skin of his hands,
deliberate in setting one thing right that day.

She goes with him on a night ship, her back to the winking
village lamplights, her father's roses unwatered, the barbed
whispers that would follow, always.

And that dainty footstep on the gangboard is the weight
of caissons crushing hop fields into history, its faltering under
the reeling stars, a near miss of their bid for the eventuality of me.

## Back to the Land

I've been there,
where the nearest neighbors were only known
by strands of chimney smoke, a community in winter
by cold air singed with the bittersweet smell of wood
burning. I have swung an axe to split logs and chopped
river ice for water when the pipes froze. Carried moths
in my apron from the kitchen, to release back inside,
because the outside was inside, everywhere.

So you are going too,
my brother, driving to Virginia, worm farm seat-belted
behind you, away to live in the vaporous greens, where
footprints of deer in grass collect the morning dew.
I know it's irresistible, the Siren song of meadowlarks
and leaf rustle in mossy-collared pines and hickory trees.

We belong more to the loamy land than to our native sand,
or each other. Decisive this leave taking, shimmying off
salt water, no turning to say I'll miss you. It's the dirt
and Nordic homesteader stuff we're made of, who choose
our pursuits of happiness, bluebirds or finches, no matter,
anywhere but here.

Now, after so many to and fros, I'm content
to let the land decide, wherever I am and ready
or not, to take me back to stay. You know I will be
easy to find in the clamor of oceans, my ear pressed
to the bark of a tree, so I can hear the murmur of sap,
surging from root to limb to leaf.

# Symmetry

   for Mayme


Between earth's gifts of gold and pearls,
and the clear glass walls of the soul, you will
always stand between light and dark, now and then,
truth and doubt.

You, the unsure, chose a carousel horse
in all its lacquered blandishments, but too circuitously
trained for the narrow ridge between two chasms.

In one, the silver strands of grandmothers' voices,
the aerial parts of herbs, the scent of sunlit water
condensing into clouds. You were sometimes volatile.

In the other, mulchy pleas of young men,
silken filaments of ragged roots upended,
the fragrance of decomposing leaves. And shreds
of owl voices at night in the windblown trees.
You were sometimes biddable.

Now hold in sight the fulcrum, that dry bit of earth
where you dropped a tiny half-moon seed, forgotten
in your dawdling time. Go gaze on that sunny field,
and you will see what you have sown, a single stalk
of hollyhock blooming with certainty,

like what you've become, a solitary blossomer
upright and lovely on the horizon, who knows
not to give up what you now possess,
to what you have lost.

# Amoretti

I. Dream

Deer come to the shade of your silence,
their black tongues probing a canopy
of leaves. I move in slowly, on all fours,
so not to startle them. "Me too,"
I say, mouth watering, "Me too."


II. Restraint

Of forbidden things I've wanted to touch
—candle flames, nettle leaves, glossy puddles
of jellyfish, your silver-stubbled jaw,
—one harbors the searing burn of all,
in touch witheld.


III. Kiss

I want you to know
that shiver was just
the last leaf falling where
you cannot see bare trees
once given to rustling
when there was only wind

# Flight Lesson

Look, you said, at the wingspan of that bird!
And then, another, a pas de deux of hawks,
unbuckled coupling, a hover in tandem,
then plummet, into the leafy shadows of home,
and what it holds.

Flushed out, a flittering bit of hawk, a fledgling
more butterfly than bird, taught by the wide-winged
master of elliptical drifts, how to fit the body to vaster
blue, and the other in partnered purpose sits as sentry,
her breast in sunlight, bright as a polished lemon.

And where we stand, on the rim of this golden field,
with what we are equipped, I know we cannot lift off,
touch wings in mid-air, make a marriage in foliage
and ether. Not there, but maybe here, earth-bound,
where winged things are but metaphors, and hawks
look down at our linked hands with suspicion.

# He's No Equestrian

No massive white horse his, on glittered hooves
No cloud-free blue sky and sundrenched arrival.
No dazzling shield, no rubied saddle leather,
nor sparkly bridle. No polished horn and brassy
scabbard over his shoulder slung. No coal black
curls nor helmet aflame with fire-red feathers.

But in the gauzy dusk, look how he cradles
in the palm of his hand, a shuddering hummingbird;
rolls sticky spider webs off tiny tips of beak, tugs
and unwinds with thumb and finger deadly threads
from wings and feet. The unblinking bird lies still,
as if in surrender to such formidable tender touches,
that lift away and adrift, the last wisps of shackle.

Then from his open hand erupts a hum, fast
the frenzied wings, high and higher, like a shred
of unfettered apparition aflutter, a small dark shape
and darkish sky merging.

And never was a man in jeans and tee shirt
on a wicker bench in faded light, so mistakable
for a Red Cross Knight.

# On Vermeer's *Woman in Blue, Reading a Letter*

His oceanic speech when he is with her, surges in waves
of ardor, and then subsides, ungraspable. Unlike the letter
she holds tight now with both hands, where her loved one
speaks in sunlit stillness with such clarion certainty
she can feel his breath on the nape of her neck.

Then there are the letters from my loved dead who arrive
like slivers of light from under closed doors, and from expired
addresses walk my corridors of memory in stockinged feet,
murmuring of morning glories, midsummer night dances
on grassy hills, harpsichord music, and cinnamon carrots,
fixed in ink.

So I will write what I want to say being here tonight,
how red wine limns a kiss, the way candle light undoes
the age in our hands, makes sfumato paintings of our faded
table flowers and day's complaints, and lay my note in a box
with brass clasps, to be released another day. Because breathed
words alone only thrive in the half life of love's eternal voice.

## Talking to Age

You lumbered into the yard one day, with a lazy sway
of your clock-pendulum tail, your great ruffled ears
the shape of the continent of Africa, idly fanning
the summer air, flicking off the ticklish feet of butterflies.
I noticed your crepey knees, and flesh sagging under
the weight of my life filled almost to capacity.

Ah Age, insidious beast, you've entered the house to stay.
Now that I can't ignore you, I should give you a room
of your own, mat the floor with hay, offer you a bowl
of peanuts, coax you to place that boulder rump more
into the corner, until I learn to trust your presence,
and those slick tusks the color of moonlight, my forklift
to heaven.

But not this room, where I sleep with one who doesn't
see you. Just a state of mind, he says. I hold his hand fiercely,
against the look of your amber eye, that ever-glowing ember
sunk in skin like ancient folds of molten lava. The searing eye
that watches me by day and by night as close as vapors
from the jungle of fear. Or as far away as my diamond-clad
contentments can push you.

# Measures of Infinity

"Just one second" according to White Rabbit,
in answer to Alice. The New York Times
Crossword said, "ends and never ends,"
meaning days. I trusted a nun who held
holy secrets, claimed it a steel ball big
as the earth, worn down to nothing
when brushed by the feather of a dove,
once in a hundred years. A telescopic mirror
let me see through 31 million light years
into an eye blue as a robin's egg,
looking back from inside a spiral
of cosmic dust frothing births of stars.
Nothing like what William Blake said.

I stumbled as he knew I would, on a grain of sand.
And right there unbidden, was Death and there too
was Love, in a blast of transparent time so fused,
I could pinch and lift it, to close in my hand.

# Remedy for the Discomforts of Writing Poems

*after a Cambodian rite from The Golden Bough*

Look for an orchid growing in shadows high on
a tamarind tree. Dress in all white, fix to your back
a clay pot, and climb the tree at dusk. Unlike you,
the orchid occupies a place of comparative security.
Break off the plant, place it in the pot, and let it drop
to the soft forest floor. Bathe the orchid in river water
and make a decoction for use by drinking or washing.
The lofty orchid will confer upon you, its fortunate
possessor, protection from the ills that beset attempts
to fit with winged words, the brittle bark and tangled
roots of life lived on the ground.

In the absence of tamarind trees, find a deep dry well,
full of the silence of nothing to say, and call into it an echo.

In the absence of orchids, watch where you walk,
for fallen lichens, and weeds that happen to cling
to the soles of your feet

In the absence of a clay pot, find a ladle, and kneel
beside a pond of dark water without reflections.
You will know what to do.

And in the absence of a white dress, undress at your
mirrored desk, and write by sunlight, where you've
watered and mulched and made meadows to grow,
full of glass-stemmed words, for the taking.

Apogee

# Shifty Words: A Sonnet

All perfect words will flee from what is meant
and so the glass is broken from the start,
recalled from its too crystalline intent,
the artifice essential to the art.
I trust less what it is than what it seems,
the smoothness of the briary path I tread,
illuminated buddha-bodied dreams
emerging from the shallows of my bed.
There is no taste of truth that does not burn
with bitter sweetness untruth on the lips.
The leaf is perforated by the worm,
opaque the unadulterated sip.
Excise the blisters from my brooding tongue:
like diamonds they will glitter in the sun.

# Annotations on Being Alone

Denotative meanings lack precision. Solitude,
for instance, as "the state of being alone".
Yearned for often when crowded too long
by one's own kind, like grass overgrown
to unbearable lushness. Balm is the spare and light,
to be everywhere at once and nowhere in particular,
alone beyond longing. A blue-sky life inside wisps
of silence, not between sounds but among them,
from spacious attics with a flutter of curtains
to the scudding clouds, and spring waterfalls
half heard in the woods.

Then there's the "sense of being alone," enclosed
in withering capacities. A marriage made of distances,
or an abandoned house that smells of damp wood.
Unseen owls at night asking your identity. The sudden
sound of a gate slammed shut by hard hands of a storm.
My neighbor's barred windows, all of them, dressed
in pink curls of iron. What must this look like from inside,
those shadows of prison windows on the floor, lengthening
with the morning sun?

A state, or sense?
No need to look up what's told
in wordless syllables from windows and wind.

# Re-formation

Once I was a star, now far from home and starish,
my shine dried and strewn about me like sand.
I sit tight, alone, so not to lose my native pools of light
in this dark and liminal space, my songs fallen
into so many cracks between cloud and rock,
rose and bone, dove and hawk. And where I lean in
to hear, things toothed and serpentine on either side.

Be brave in your worth and ask, is that dissonance
music misunderstood? Celestial bodies burn and freeze,
melt and break, change the weather, yet turn close
and apart in equal measure, and hum to us
their spherical tune from the moment of our birth.
So let us sit together unboxed, shape a new betweenness
in the cradle of a curve, and listen there awhile.

# Mary

The stars are fallen from my head,
the moon is parted from my feet
I have restored my mantle to the sun.
It is done, the pitting of my prayers
Against the stench of serpent's breath.
I am old, and dust crusts my sandals. Humanly,

I wander hand in hand with dusk, where troughs
and peaks of hills in coolness lie, sheep sleep
on their knees, and all are softened into shadows
under the lowering blanket of heaven.

# Reasons for Shoes

Like slant-toothed escalators, hot asphalt,
muddy snow. Gritty deserts and corrugated
canyons, or simply red-soled vanity.

Until there comes a slipshod day where
the edge of the ocean meets a satin-sanded
beach, and the ache for expansion is so urgent,
shoes are safe to abandon. For reasons,
as Rilke said, *like walking on fishes.*

Or waiting on the cozy side of the door
to a Chinese restaurant, two girls and
their fathers, mine gliding me to our seats,
hers begging for food. Her tiny white toes
exposed in pink plastic high heeled shoes
with sparkles, so pretty, and the night so cold.
In socks, I felt an uneasy pang of warmth.

She slipped away for reasons,
but left her shoes for me, on the floor
of my memory, and wherever she fled,
after so many years, I hold those hard
glittered shoes in thrall, wet with salt water.

# Where Girls May Go

Our hair tameless as tumbleweeds, we hurtled into canyons,
and stood to pedal on bikes bought big for growing into.

Boys had more fun it seemed, and so we shunned our dolls
for dusty shoes and scabby knees. We smelled of sage,
and sported stabs of cactus thorns. Built forts, soared
on rope swings over rocked ravines.

But there came a day, when Susie and I rolled up to John's garage,
where boys played pool. And she appeared, his sudden mother,
soft-faced in the chimerical blur of adulthood, her dark hair
wrested into a taut French twist. She extended one leg,
nylon-stockinged and flawless, tilted her foot to the seam
of the driveway, her high-heeled shoe pointed as a rapier.
She drew a line with her toe, and said,

"No girls beyond here."

And Susie's brother, Rudy, the one who helped us build
rafts for our dogs to ride on the pond, leaned on his cue stick,
hand over hand like a prophet, and grinned crookedly, as if to say,
"So be it."

We grew into junior high, wearing white socks and loafers
polished like gleaming mahogany, our Suave-washed hair
pinched into ponytails, and budding breasts arrested
by Maidenform.

One morning, we watched John in our classroom
window light, and the girl with glossy sausage curls,
velvet ribbons, and merciless black-seed eyes, hand back
some trinket of affection, a bracelet, maybe.

We felt the falling of leaden petals, saw the blush of anguish
in a boy's face, the forbidden limits a girl met with disdain,
and no stone, steel, nor spear-sharp shoe could stop her crossing.

# Shadow Horses

My grandmother rode her horse out to me from her bed.
I was on my way to places far from Texas, her wooden house,
and purple curtains. Places I could not write home about on
postcards of cathedrals; that would make the horned toad I once
carried in a Dixie cup from Amarillo, a souvenir of paradise.

The hills were lavender, her red hair bounty, and he rode beside
her, the man whose rakish face hangs in the hallway, whose black
eyes squint a dare-you look a woman with a good horse would take
the highest ledge for.

"I don't want to die," she whispered. "I know," I said. As if
the noon day sun overhead had riveted my horse alongside hers,
to nibble grass in a fondling breeze. As if our knees were crisp
as biscuits, and we smelled of sage, and had paused to see just
how far we could spit. As if the pitch and girth of time did not
resist such easy knowing.

She went her way. And I went mine, hurtling on a Greyhound bus
into a night not one star could pierce, eyes wide open to see
anything at all. Somewhere near Raton, a ventriloquist unpacked
his dummy to practice that old routine of throwing voices
in the dark, where no one listens, and the ride has been so long,
we take our shadows for ourselves.

# Almost Grief

The dead who loved me
would not want writhing vines
of thorns to clutch my heart,

the fire of regrets for what can't
be taken back to scorch my dreams,
spite to bloom a noxious purpling
in my eyes where clean tears should well.

They would not want soft fruits
of forgiveness to turn to gristle
in my mouth, a drink of memories
to taste of nightshade on my tongue,

stigmata on my hands to hold a thing
they once had touched, or my bare feet
to bleed on cactus carpets in familiar woods
of kinship.

But there was one who didn't.

# En Passant

Here's that old blue sky and open road again, famous
for its mandate to fit mute beauties of the world
with words; and a ready muse, stirring futilely, captive
of such air and light and bright horizons, as make
parallel perspective for the soul in search of runways.

But here comes a flatbed truck, sidling up,
flaunting hot orange cones, suggesting dust and asphalt
as the stuff of rabid love, before it fades from view,
having no time to wait for a poem in the clutches of succor.

# Consolation for Lost Love

You will hear a gathering hum, the voices of your friends,
as they swarm in rank and file around you, like a flock
straight from the court of Fra Angelico's glorifying angels
gowned in shell pink, grass green, dusty red, and windy blue,
with freckled pheasant wings, gemmy halos, and silver slippers.

They will make you almost glad to be so bitter, when they offer
jeweled flasks of liquor distilled from rue and wormwood,
for your pleasure.

There will also be one who holds for you a sweeter remedy,
the clear water of forgiveness in a crystal vial, sealed
with lake-blue wax. You are not obliged to drink it.
And only if you don't will your band of angels hover
slant-wise overhead.

Stay put, and you will feel the soothing balm,
their celestial ever-readiness to nourish your bias.

# He Said

"You look pretty today." And I made some plans:
To fly to Rome with red roses for Keats' grave.
To dance on a beach swathed in moonlit surf,
stars so near as to settle winking in my hair.
To own a Chesapeake Bay retriever with sky blue
eyes and a velvet chocolate coat. To wear
a saffron sari and adopt a child from Bangladesh.
To make that three-tiered Black Forest cake from
the recipe scrawled on my organ donor card.
To return to those woods in Vermont, where
snow water hurls itself downhill in spring,
and applauds in the ecstasy of falling. To lie
on soft moss among curly fiddleheads of ferns.

But I am stuck in traffic on Park Boulevard,
watching a prostitute. She smiles uncertainly,
at no one in particular, bronze skin drawn taut
across the high bones of her cheeks, white-sweatered
breasts jutting at angles to tempt and defy. A wad
of scarf grips her throat like an animal, and bus fumes
turn her to vapor where she stands.

Someone please tell her, before the sun goes down,
before the night engulfs her with impossibilities,
"You look pretty today."

# Unweeding

Weeds make level ground lumpy. I wanted to clear them
from sight, ensure no re-emergence. Slash the clover's webbed
anchors, yank out the seedy grass, tenacious roots of dandelions,
and invasive memories of my mother's face when I told her I was
too busy to talk, that same face paralysis made forever speechless.

When gardeners pulled up the poppy sprouts, ferny trespassers
among shrubs, and roughed over the gashed earth with bark,
I fell to my knees. If only I could claw that ground deep enough
to drag back my every gone and forgotten loved thing.

Or if I wept away regrets there long enough to coax up volunteers,
I could unforget the rejected weeds I need.

# A Taste of Tangerine

You are folded in your wheeled chair, remote
as a roosting pelican. A perpetual half smile
seals in your tranquility. It is too late for me
to learn again to call you Daddy, a cartoon name,
like a rumpled birthday hat I cannot make you wear.

Still, because you ask, I try the tangerines,
tote the picker to the tree. The top one, you insist,
enmeshed in leaves. The rigid limbs resist, raining
debris. I twist the iron fingers, tear fiercely, make
the capture, a caged color raging in the sky. It nestles
in my hand like a wounded bird, skin ripped, flesh bared.
I peel away the velvet veins, touch the juice with my tongue.
It is an acrid Pyrrhic victory and you have exited, coasted
out on the smooth decks of things, heading for the silent rim
of the horizon, to feed on manna that falls from heaven,
before I can tell you: The tangerines are not ready to eat.

And I being prone to love, will wait without pickers,
Among gnarled roots, for bitter fruit to ripen into sweet.

# Okanagan Cradling Time

Golden mornings, on the back porch steps,
I sat with you yet unborn, and the poems
of William Blake. The wakened fields shimmered
with dew, and the chattering rooks, high up
in the Quaking Aspen trees I asked to be still.
Listen, I said.

"Who made thee? Dost thou know who made thee?
Gave thee life and bid thee feed . . . gave thee clothing
of delight, softest clothing wooly bright."
Purple shadows stirred among sunlit leaves
in answer to assertions of innocence.

And in the small dark sea my body made for you,
my amphibian lamb, you slumbered safe and warm
in your watery dreams.

So safe, a little while more.

# Not Now Keats's Autumn

Easy to love leavings when young, hair winnowed by wind
and mind drowsed with the fume of youth in bud, and budding
more. When warm days never ceased, all fruits ripened to the core,
and always later flowers for bees. If buds dropped or seeds failed,
summer was overbrimmed, and less surfeit not missed.

Not now's losings, age's unleafing, loves upon loves fluttered
to ground, self-worth shrunk, and the last oozings of time's sap
by days, then hours by hours, until the body, light as a gnat,
mourns to be borne or sunk as the wind lifts or dies.
Or rejoices released as mist adrift and seasonless.

# Fractal Homily

If the lonely Creator of the world were to choose
a new, more accessible name, surely it would be Zinnia.
Beguilingly spiraled, and prone to grow on the borders
of existence, seen first and last by the young and old.
Also through fissures in the time between:

Where cooking pudding bubbles up dark moths
that light sticky-winged on the walls and ceiling.
Where candles are lit for dinner and the flames freeze
hard as ice, and all there is for salad are leaves of yew.
Where bedroom windows will not close, and cold rain
causes the empty laced nightgown on a bedpost to shudder.
Where silken pillows are laid for dreams on graveled ground,
and bees cluster in the salty streams of tears. Where efforts
fail to reassemble storm-scattered bird nests from a bucket,
and selves like dandelions shiver in hiding from the wind.

There in drafty crevices, Zinnia unfolds the golden ratio
of its corolla. Longing to be recognized and rendered
as a child does, crayon in fist, stem straight up, petals
upon petals, radiant in everything.

Earthshine

# Stoical Gardening

The passionflower is not at all philosophical.
It flings a spirograph of purple threads, opens
its lemony wheel of pollen pouches to a naturalist
who doesn't have the wing-beat of a three thousandth
of an ounce fuzzed body, for one buzzy shuffle dance
on pistils and stamens.

A stoical gardener controls what she can, and ignores
the rest, like the rain forest-mined pink sapphires
in the lobes of her ears.

When she saw it going, thoughts of possible loss
excited delight awhile in the long-gone bee.
And now there's a duty to be useful.

She takes a brush and scissors from flower to flower.
Tickles anther tips where grains of pollen stick.
Or cuts a bundle for pushing, unnaturally, but poetic.

Outside a poem, nothing leafy needs to fill the deeps
of human longing. The vine will be itself.
Without our hunger, its perfumed fruit incidental.
Still, a poem needs our need for leafless namings,
to remediate where possible, the ache of vacancies.

# From the Altar of the Northern White Rhinos

Come into the vanishing, see our likeness,
not to boulders sunk in mountain slopes,
but to vestal virgins, keepers of what flames
are left of our kind, whose unborn children
of the lost fathers are extinguished now.

Under acacia tree umbrellas, in the tabernacles
of our bodies, a sacred language ages-old
as silky sweet tastes of the cream of the moon
or honey of the sun on a root of white yam,
scriptures doomed upon metallic tongues
of machetes.

And this is medicine, not our pinnacled horn
powdered into tea, but the shiver of an ear
to the sudden hiss of dry grass. The deep drink
of speckled pebbles and shreds of clouds
in the mirror of a lake. To be at ease, not enmity,
with our dwelling place.

Where all our delicate threads of breath are woven:
tortoise, skylark, pine tree, human, into slip knots.

# Habitats

Where floors crack and melt from under the feet
of penguins, and Madagascar forest walls, slashed
and burnt, scatter lemurs to flee without foliage
or branches to cling to. Where sea turtles lose
coral reefs to hide from the severing theft
of their shells for décor.

Where with the trusty construction kit
of a child's imagination, I made a house of boxes
on the backyard lawn, so to sleep untethered from
the monotony of a warm bed. As midnight dew
seeped into cardboard, and my ceiling sagged
and slumped, I breathed the sweet rancid smell
of freedom, and knew I was not ready for its threats.

But near me was a window glowing golden
in the dark, and I could choose to go inside.

# Death of the Sweet Peas: A Love Story

"It was magical to see the flowers die naturally," she said.
This from a friend who loved the sweet peas escaped
from garden walls, that tumbled down slopes by the sea.

Let live the sun-drunk pastel riot, silky coy coils
unfurled, pinkish petals sipped by breezes, and when spent,
rained seeds to bloom in Spring again, and Spring again.

Until the ruffled revelry brought love come running
from novelties of redwoods, and arctic tundras.
Ardent love as underfoot crushes, or as clutches
a crowd redoubles, sweet peas grasped by fistfuls
into chaff.

And the ocean wind, thirsty for candied fragrance,
whispers to bristles of hillside thatch, what is loved
enough, cannot be held too close, too long, too much.

# Large Language and Smashing Rocks

There's talk of a new Intelligence that advances
collecting patterns, and delivers all of a sudden,
re-wrapped old knowing, from, well, everything known.
Sometimes it wears a silicon human face devoid of longing,
or knowing what to long for, such as breaks in dark places.
Not like cracks in mud sundried after rain, but openings
to never-before light: a cure for perpetual pain, the gift
of forgiveness for guilt, affection for a sealed heart.

And the lure of curiosity, where in the canyon as a child,
I broke with a bigger rock a drab rock, and saw it burst
into snowy crusts of crystals, a deep-faceted glassy dazzle
blazing back to the sun, new light. My language then was not
large enough for "astonishment" but I knew what it was
and in the ordinary, ever after, sought it.

## Inseparable

Once we were free as fish in the sea, full as the sea in the fish.
We knew and moved with currents of wind, and seasonal shifts.
Hills and lowlands softened under our feet, into paths wherever
necessity led. Forest canopies sheltered our backs and dropped
gems of sunlight in the shade where we slept.

War declared on the tired, the poor, the huddled masses,
is war on us: Polish lynx, West Bank gazelle, American ocelot.

We cannot que up to wait at gates for a pool of water,
become entangled in razor wire for access to pastures, or clamber
for mates just within reach on the other side of electric fences.

When our jeweled dreams are dissolved by search lights,
we thirst for a shared quaff of moonlight, impartial as rain,
that runs like a river seeking the ocean, and pours into
all our vessels of bone, blood, heart, and brain.

# Coyote Reditus

Regal golden jackal, deity before Quetzalcoatl,
God's dog, is not yours the kingdom of chaparral,
sage and sumac, the canyon ledge your choir loft?
Where is your voice tonight?

The stars once stooped to roof you, and the moon,
your courtesan, whose fingers plied the ruff
of your neck, whose face swam in the pools
of your eyes, whose dropped shawl made canopies
of manzanita, for your sleep. To her, you hurled your
wild rhapsodies.

Then some said, scour the land to make backyards
for apple trees, and pave what's left with asphalt.
Now, only captive dogs, with no sky music
in their throats, shriek from behind locked doors.

So, old protean trickster, you are caught in traffic.
A lone lean-limbed dancer, you crouch and trot,
dodge a crush of horns and wheels, headlights
igniting white flares in your eyes.

And just before dawn, a fat cat's gone missing,
and some windfall fruit. We hold our breath,
the moon and I, to hear your riff on victory
startle up the sun.

# To Live in the World

> *. . . you must learn to play like a fox.*
> —Machiavelli

Another day dropped into the leaden dust
of unremembered acts. Was it something said,
or unsaid? A task there was no time for,
or gone unnoticed?

When across the gulf between what is free,
and what is not, I met a fox in grassy vapor
Long looks mean fear or love, and I was not
afraid. I wanted to learn how to trot through
ditches and gardens cobbled with melons, glide
over deadfalls, and twitch an ear to the earth's
secluded music, foot-scratch of quail,
and the murmur of wind in maple leaves.

I could make a nest of my body in the shelter
of meadow shadows, the moon's light on my back,
silvering untroubled sleep. Chances are the roadside
would, in time, wear me like a scab, but if it all comes
down to scrambled bones, in the sum of things,
the best survival owes debt to play.

# Equation

What does this add to the sum of life?
Golden milkweed planted under wooly lanterns
of purple buddleia, and open red lips of salvia;
a chubby citron larvae body intrepidly striped;
five ordeals of shed skins; only moments in a lusty
leaf-munching instar self before the wished-for
chrysalis dangles flat and death crisped.

Or bursts of cadmium orange and black,
white confetti freckled; those Tiffany mosaic
wings clasped shut on the ground like a tilting sail
a breeze caused to stammer, never again unfurl?
(I buried it wrapped in hollyhock leaves,
tied with twine in a bow.)

But that there begins one more ascent of stem,
a twilight green enclosure, a jittery spinning flight.
And a wing-stirred spoonful of air launches a storm.

# Fields and Trees

This is the field electric, magnetic energy skeins of longings
clutched in a cyber shuttle that weaves unseen, a tapestry
of circadian Netflix binges, cherished Facebook friends unmet,
detritus of texts spilled into cell phones, and digital music into
the solitary confinement of earbuds.

But here, a young apple tree shoves ruddy fruit into every nook
of its untried branches. Boughs of juniper, shaggy musicians
of wind by day, and under early evening stars, soft dollops
of shadows where nestle dreaming bodies of doves.
And a Kashmir Cypress, gentle arms in silken foliage like
the fringe of a pashmina shawl, open to passersby all, as if kin.

To be heard and known. Wishes of trees too, though virtual
agitations dampen the deep earthen hum of our roots,
the sky-faced leaves of our listening.

# The Way to Eat a Pomegranate

Parched and palled is best, after summer,
and full of your original sin. Approach
your tree in autumn light, when slant-sunned
guilt gilds tangled branches, elliptical leaves,
and splintered secrecies. Reach through, seize
the apple's afterword, Eden's recompense,
a glossy globe of mottled rubiness.
Not easy fruit, but merciful, so wrest it free.
Its upside-down crown let rest in your palm.
Open it by any means. Find to eat a wet nest
of red gems. The bitter seeds to chew,
the desperate thirst to slake. Let the soothing
incarnadine juice trickle down, and re-paint
the life in your face.

# To Love a "Super Mutt"

. . . what a DNA test said of him, not a shred of hoped-for
aristocracy, just more hidden past.

You aren't dreaming the stealthy advance that wakes you
from sleep, his belly on your belly, eyes glossy as molasses
pouring into yours.

He tells you Lord Byron taught him to go no more a-roving
so late into the night to howl with coyotes at the moon
so still and bright.

How calmed he feels to slip inside deep shadows of a car,
as he once snuck into a barrel and rolled over Niagara Falls.

That chasing his tail is the meditative practice he learned
from a homeless Sufi dervish in Central Park.

And his tail wags to the beat of a Mariachi band he heard
when lost in the streets of Guadalajara.

If he says he was a Theosophist, learned mental telepathy
from Madame Blavatsky, and used it to lure you
to his concrete-floored shelter cage,

believe him. And when he trembles, hold him tight.

## How to Rock and Roll with God

What is the joy of moonlight-glazed grass untouched
by bare toes, or scents of roses without the lingering
nose of a shabby-sweatered passerby?

Knowing the adenine and thymine of your DNA are in
that eucalyptus tree, may urge you to feel its circumference.
Go ahead, no one's looking, and with your arms take
measure before its immigrant kind are felled from
that native plants preserve.

If you forgot the way to move to the tune of rain, tilt up
your face, eyes closed, imagined feathers sleeked, and let
ribbons of water slide over the slopes of your body. Or open
your mouth like an African drought-shrunk lake, refilling.

Go low, to the secret spore dwellings in gills
of mushrooms, under fronds of bracken, and flanges
of pinecones, their hidden escapes for survival revealed
to you who don't need to leave home to thrive.

You can't rock and roll with God, he said.
But when Little Richard threw his diamonds in the river,
oh the sunlit glitter, the scintillation of what flows
within over half of you.

# About the Author

Carrie Weinberger's immersion in visual art as a graduate of the Rhode Island School of Design, and director of educational programming at the Hood Museum of Art at Dartmouth College, inform her pleasure in painting with words. Her poems have appeared in numerous literary journals, and she was a nominee for the Pushcart Prize. She lives and writes in Carlsbad, California.

www.ingramcontent.com/pod-product-compliance
Lightning Source LLC
Chambersburg PA
CBHW030915170426
43193CB00009BA/861